Thanks,
Mom

from _____

_____

Thanks, Mom

ST. MARTIN'S PRESS

NEW YORK

ALSO BY ALLEN APPEL

Thanks, Dad
From Father to Son

Editor: Jared Kieling
Production Editor: David Stanford Burr
Design: Henry Sene Yee

ISBN 0-312-10557-6

First Edition: April 1994
10 9 8 7 6 5 4 3 2 1

Thanks, Mom

THANKS MOM,

for . . .

_____

First of all, the big one.

Thanks for
carrying me for nine months
and going through the pain of bringing me
into the world. Without that there
would be nothing else.
But you did, and there was,
and so...

Continuing
to lug me around for the next
several years.

Feeding me.
Burping me.
Holding me.
Bathing me.
Changing all those diapers.

THANKS MOM, *for*...

_____

———————————

Getting up at night,
year after year, for a host of reasons,
from simple feedings and basic comforting
to true emergencies.

And all the while being patient
and kind.

THANKS MOM, *for...*

Singing to me.

Kissing me.

Dressing me warmly and
making sure my head was covered
so my brain
didn't catch cold.

Holding my hand.

Teaching me how to walk.

Picking me up when I fell.

Stuffing
me into snowsuits
until I looked like Poppin' Fresh,
The Pillsbury Doughboy.
I couldn't move around so well,
but boy was I warm.

Keeping track of my mittens.

Making snowmen with me.

Showing me how to make a snow angel.

Not yelling at me for eating snow
even though,
as you pointed out a number of times,
there was always the possibility that
a dog had peed on it.

Smiling.

Lifting me up.

L etting Dad
toss me up in the air and catch me,
even though it made you
nervous.

Making me eat my vegetables.

Making silly airplane noises so I would
eat my vegetables.

Letting me
keep all my small toys
even though Dad would sometimes
step on them in the middle of the night
in his bare feet
and swear he was going to throw them
all away.

———————

Putting up with some
world-class temper tantrums.

Tying my shoes.

Feeling my forehead and instantly knowing
if I was coming down with
something.

Wiping my nose.

THANKS MOM, *for...*

Making me take my medicine,
and thinking up clever ways to disguise it so
I could get it down.

Getting me
drinks of water in the middle of
the night.

THANKS MOM, *for . . .*

Getting up at night
and nursing me through colic,
earaches, stopped-up noses, upset stomachs,
chicken pox, measles, colds, flus,
and a hundred other
sometimes undiagnosed, undefined,
aches, pains, and diseases
that ran the gamut
from trivial to life-threatening.

THANKS MOM, *for*...

———————————————

Reading to me.

THANKS MOM, *for...*

_____

———————————

Worrying,
worrying, worrying, worrying.

Worrying.

Cleaning up
God-knows-how-many messes
of every size, shape,
and description.

Changing the sheets
so the bed was crisp and cool when I was
hot and tired.

Cool washcloths.

THANKS MOM, *for...*

Chicken noodle soup.

Ginger ale
with ice cubes
in a glass.

Saltine crackers.

Letting me out of bed when I felt better,
even though I probably should have
stayed down for another day.

And through all those sicknesses,
never showing how frightened you
sometimes were.

THANKS MOM, *for . . .*

Cooking,
cooking, cooking,
day after day, year after year,
always trying to
make it healthy
and interesting.

*(Except some of the time,
when you gave in and
let us eat junk.)*

Keeping the house clean,

with my help.

Washing the dishes.

And letting me dry.

Playing a million games.
In particular,
Concentration, Old Maid, Checkers,
Go Fish, Slap Jack, War,
and Crazy Eights.

THANKS MOM, *for . . .*

Not allowing me to cheat.

Never "letting" me win.

(except once in a while)

THANKS MOM, *for...*

Making us
sit back from the TV
so we wouldn't soak up too many of the
deadly rays.
I'm sure this saved our lives.

Making up stories.

THANKS MOM, *for . . .*

Saving
my artistic efforts and
putting them up on the refrigerator
for all the world
to see.

THANKS MOM, *for . . .*

———————————————

Taking us to the park.

Taking us to the playground.

THANKS MOM, *for . . .*

———————

Helping me pack my bags
when I decided to run away from home,
and not making fun of me
when I changed
my mind.

THANKS MOM, *for*...

Letting me use
public restrooms by myself,
even though it made you
nervous.

Checking under
the bed and in the closet
for monsters and
vampire bats.

THANKS MOM, *for...*

―――――――――

Taking me trick or treating.

Checking

my candy carefully so I didn't

eat any pins or razors.

THANKS MOM, *for . . .*

———————————

Making
a thousand costumes,
from Halloween to school plays,
to backyard fairs.

———————

Washing mountains of dirty clothes.

Putting clean sheets on my bed.

THANKS MOM, *for...*

Mending holes and sewing on
buttons.

Kidding me.

Being fair,
even though I often thought
you weren't.

Admiring just about everything that
I did.

THANKS MOM, *for* . . .

_____

Buying me
new sneakers, dress shoes, and all the
clothes over the years.

THANKS MOM, *for* . . .

_____

Christmas.

Everything about Christmas.

Making sure
I always gave Grandma and Grandpa
a kiss and a hug.

Making me
spend time with all of
my relatives.

Even the boring ones.

Getting me
together
with all
of my cousins.

_____

Helping
take care of the parade of pets that
marched through our house
year after year.

———————

Making me help around the house.

Pretending that I was actually helping
around the house.

Fixing lunch for
all the neighborhood kids.

Not making fun of me
when I decided that
my room
was haunted.

—————————————

Explaining things.

Being patient.

Making me take piano lessons.

Making me practice.

Letting me quit.

Not telling Dad
quite a few things when he came home
at night.

Keeping your temper.

Most of the time.

Making me laugh.

Helping me with my homework.

Drilling me on:

Spelling

Addition

Subtraction

Multiplication

Division

Historic dates

State capitals

_____

Driving me a million places:
friends' houses, the library, the mall,
to school when it rained, and
generally all over town.

Not

crying when

I went away to summer camp.

Not being

too overjoyed when

I went away to summer camp.

THANKS MOM, *for...*

Letting me go to the movies alone
with my friends.

THANKS MOM, *for...*

_____

Admitting it when you were wrong and
I was right.

(Seldom, I admit.)

Not pretending to know things that
you didn't know.

Teaching me to "look it up."

Sticking up

for me at school when I got in trouble

but

was in the right.

Being reasonably good humored,
or at least resigned about
my report cards.

_____

Teaching me to ride a bike.

Letting me sleep out in the backyard
at least once a summer.

Convincing
me in a grown-up way
that I really didn't need a horse,
nor could we reasonably stable one
in the backyard.

Getting

all dressed up on special occasions.

Teaching me that
"all the other kids have them"
wasn't a good reason for
buying things.

THANKS MOM, *for...*

Making me take my vitamins.

THANKS MOM, *for*...

———————————————

Never forgetting my birthday,
and always making
a cake.

THANKS MOM, *for...*

———————

Hot chocolate on snowy days.
With marshmallows.

Bedtime snacks.

Cooking:

Chocolate chip cookies

Doughnuts

Fried chicken

Pies

_____

Taking me
to the emergency room on
more than a few occasions.
And remaining calm so
I wouldn't be
scared.

Buying me books,

even though

we couldn't afford them.

Buying me lots of things,

even though

we couldn't afford them.

THANKS MOM, *for...*

Not yelling at me too much.

Not
changing your mind.
Changing your mind when it was really
important to me,
even though you said you wouldn't.

Convincing Dad
to change his mind.

THANKS MOM, *for . . .*

———————

Making sure
I had a decent breakfast every day
before I went to school.

Encouraging me.

Discouraging me, when needed.

Letting me keep
my light on at night so
I could read just
a little longer.

THANKS MOM, *for . . .*

————————

Teaching me
the value of telling the truth.

Teaching me good manners.

Nagging,
but not too much, and only when
I needed it.

———————————

Letting me go to the library
whenever I said I really needed to.

Always seeing me in a good light.

Letting me pick out
my own clothes.

Making sure I was
presentable,
most of the time.

Not laughing out loud
at the fashions I,
and most the
other kids my age,
were prey to.

Pretending
not to notice when I was acting
like an idiot.

Understanding
that there were just some things
I couldn't talk about
with you.

THANKS MOM, *for...*

———————

Making me study.

Letting me
stay up late on the weekends.

Letting me
sleep in on Saturday mornings.

Not being unbearable about
good grades.

Laughing at my jokes.

Cheering me up when I was disappointed.

Being there
when I needed you.
Quietly, unobtrusively, undeniably.
Always.

THANKS MOM, *for...*

_____

Teaching me how to parallel park.

Letting me drive the car.

Not complaining about my driving
when you were
a passenger.

_____

Making me get a summer job.

Making me save part of the money
I earned.

Not criticizing how I spent the money
I earned.

THANKS MOM, *for...*

———————

Interceding with Dad, throughout the years.

Not making fun of
my kinds of music.

Laughing.

Not laughing.

At the
blessed Grotto
I have

prayed for you.

At the
blessed Grotto
I have
prayed for you.

Letting me keep
my room pretty much the way
I wanted to.

Making me clean up my room when
it really needed it.

THANKS MOM, *for...*

Not listening
when I talked to special friends
on the telephone.

Teaching me
that you never drink and drive,
or ride in a car with a drunk
behind the wheel.

Even if you have to walk home.

THANKS MOM, *for . . .*

Not inquiring
too closely as to where I had been
when I was out at night.

THANKS MOM, *for...*

Teaching me how to wash
my own clothes.

Teaching me how to iron.

THANKS MOM, *for...*

Teaching me how to take
care of myself.

Being proud of me.

THANKS MOM, *for*...

——————————

Holding on.

THANKS MOM, *for...*

———————————

L   e   t   t   i   n   g

THANKS MOM, *for*...

_____

g   o   .

THANKS MOM, *for...*

_____

_____

_____

_____

_____

_____

_____

THANKS MOM, *for* . . .

_____

_____

_____

_____

_____

_____